The Women's Institute

one-pot
dishes

the**WI**
INSPIRING WOMEN

SIMON &
SCHUSTER
ILLUSTRATED

London · New York · Sydney · Toronto · New Delhi
A CBS COMPANY

First published in Great Britain by Simon
& Schuster UK Ltd, 2012
A CBS Company

Simon & Schuster Illustrated Books,
Simon & Schuster UK Ltd,
222 Gray's Inn Road, London WC1X 8HB

www.simonandschuster.co.uk

Simon & Schuster Australia, Sydney
Simon & Schuster India, New Delhi

1 3 5 7 9 10 8 6 4 2

Editorial Director: **Francine Lawrence**
Senior Commissioning Editor: **Nicky Hill**
Project Editor: **Nicki Lampon**
Designer: **Richard Proctor**
Photographer: **William Shaw**
Stylist and Art Direction: **Tony Hutchinson**
Home Economist: **Sara Lewis**
Commercial Director: **Ami Richards**
Production Manager: **Katherine Thornton**

Colour reproduction by Dot Gradations Ltd, UK
Printed and bound in China

A CIP catalogue record for this book is available
from the British Library

ISBN 978-1-47110-177-9

Notes on the recipes

Both metric and imperial measurements have
been given in all recipes. Use one set of
measurements only and not a mixture of both.
Spoon measures are level and 1 tablespoon =
15 ml, 1 teaspoon = 5 ml.

Preheat ovens before use and cook on the centre
shelf unless cooking more than one item. If using
a fan oven, reduce the heat by 10–20°C, but
check with your handbook.

Medium eggs have been used unless otherwise
stated.

This book contains recipes made with nuts.
Those with known allergic reactions to nuts
and nut derivatives, pregnant and breast-feeding
women and very young children should avoid
these dishes.

Recipes in this book were first published in
2002 under the titles *Best-kept Secrets of the
Women's Institute: Low Fat Family Cooking*,
*Best-kept Secrets of the Women's Institute: Low
Calorie Home Cooking*, *Best-kept Secrets of the
Women's Institute: Healthy Heart*, *Best-kept
Secrets of the Women's Institute: Healthy Fast
Food* and *Best-kept Secrets of the Women's
Institute: Home Cooking*.

Contents

Introduction

Nothing beats home cooking. Homemade meals have so much more flavour and goodness in them than ready-made meals from the supermarket. And nothing brings family and friends together more than sitting down to a special meal that has been made with fresh ingredients and love. But many people see home cooking as time consuming and requiring lots of different equipment. This book from the Women's Institute – an absolute authority on home cooking – is here to prove the opposite, that you can cook a delicious meal in just one pot.

Soups and casseroles, curries and bakes – wonderful meals for all sorts of occasions and all cooked in just one pan, dish or pot. One-pot meals help to ease the hassle – simpler to prepare, fewer pots and pans to juggle with and obviously less washing up at the end!

Although many of these recipes are quick to cook and ideal for after work, others are perfect for days when you have a little more time and can leave a meal to simmer slowly on the hob or in the oven while you get on with other things. Not just for family dinners either, these are delicious meals that are great for entertaining too. Even kids will love a Sausage & Lentil Casserole (see page 76) or entertain your friends with the delicious Beef in Red Wine (see page 60).

Stock up your store cupboard with the basics and then you'll just need a few fresh ingredients to get going. All of these recipes are easy to make and tasty too. And with the backing of the Women's Institute you can't go wrong.

Simple
soups

Minestrone soup

Serves 4–6
Preparation and
cooking time:
55 minutes

1 tablespoon **olive oil**
115 g (4¼ oz) **pancetta** or
    rindless **back bacon**,
    snipped into pieces
1 **leek**, finely sliced
1 **carrot**, peeled and diced
1 **celery stick**, finely sliced
1 large **onion**, finely
    chopped
400 g can **chopped**
    tomatoes
1.4 litres (2½ pints) good-
    quality **vegetable, ham**
    or **chicken stock**
1 **bay leaf**
1 tablespoon **tomato purée**
½ x 410 g can **cannellini** or
    butter beans, drained and
    rinsed
50 g (1¾ oz) small **pasta**
a handful of fresh **basil**
    leaves, torn
salt and freshly ground
    black pepper
175 g (6 oz) **Savoy cabbage**
    or **spring greens**,
    shredded
finely grated **Parmesan**
    cheese, to garnish
    (optional)

Heat the oil in a large lidded saucepan. Add the pancetta or bacon, leek, carrot, celery and onion. Toss them in the oil, cover and leave to sweat over a low heat for 10 minutes, without browning. Shake the pan occasionally.

Add the tomatoes, stock, bay leaf and tomato purée. Bring to the boil, cover and simmer for 20 minutes.

Add the beans, pasta and basil. Season and return to the boil. Simmer for another 10 minutes, or until the pasta is cooked.

Three minutes before the end of the cooking time, add the cabbage or spring greens to the pan, cover and allow it to steam on top of the soup. Stir through the cabbage or greens and serve with a bowl of Parmesan, if using, for guests to add themselves.

Tip Minestrone is usually finished off with a generous topping of grated Parmesan. Personally, I feel that this rather 'takes over' from the subtle flavour of the vegetables. As a compromise, hand round a bowl of freshly grated Parmesan for those who feel that the soup needs it.

Variation Vary the vegetables according to the season – for instance, substitute courgettes or spinach for the cabbage during the summer months.

Spiced sweet potato soup

The hint of chilli powder and cumin makes this a warming soup for the cooler days of autumn and winter.

Serves 6
Preparation time: 35 minutes
Cooking time: 20 minutes

1 tablespoon **olive oil**, plus extra to garnish
1 **onion**, chopped
2 **garlic cloves**, crushed
2 **red peppers**, de-seeded and diced
250 g (9 oz) **sweet potato**, peeled and diced
350 g (12 oz) **vine-tomatoes**, de-seeded and roughly chopped
a pinch of **chilli powder**
½ teaspoon **ground cumin**
850 ml (1½ pints) **vegetable stock**
½ teaspoon **caster sugar**
freshly ground **black pepper**
fresh **basil leaves**, to garnish (optional)

Heat the olive oil in a large lidded saucepan and gently cook the onion and garlic for 5 minutes until softened but not browned. Stir in the red peppers, sweet potato and tomatoes, along with the chilli powder and cumin. Cook for a further 5 minutes to soften the vegetables.

Pour in the stock, bring up to the boil, reduce the heat and then cover and leave to simmer for 20 minutes until the vegetables are tender.

Allow the soup to cool a little and then, using a blender or food processor, purée the soup in batches until smooth. Pass the soup through a sieve to remove any small pieces of tomato skin and return it to the rinsed-out saucepan. Stir in the sugar and check the seasoning, adding some freshly ground black pepper, if desired.

Gently reheat the soup, then serve immediately in warmed bowls, garnishing with a drizzle of olive oil and fresh basil, if using.

Tip Using vine tomatoes, although slightly more expensive, really enhances the flavour of the soup.

Hot tomato soup

The little bit of chilli gives this soup a warming glow. If you wish, serve garnished with basil or chopped parsley and accompany with a cheesy bread.

Serves 4
**Preparation time: 20
  minutes**
**Cooking time:
  20 minutes**

1 tablespoon **olive oil**
1 **onion**, chopped
1 **carrot**, peeled and sliced
½ fat **red chilli**, de-seeded
  and finely chopped
400 g can **chopped
  tomatoes**
about 600 ml (20 fl oz)
  good **vegetable**, **ham** or
  chicken stock
1 **bay leaf**
½ teaspoon **brown sugar**
salt and freshly ground
  black pepper

Heat the oil in a large lidded saucepan. Stir in the onion, carrot and chilli. Cover the pan and leave the vegetables to sweat over a low heat for 5 minutes, without browning. Shake the pan occasionally.

Add the tomatoes, stock, bay leaf and sugar. Season to taste. Bring to the boil, reduce the heat, cover and simmer for 20 minutes, until the vegetables are cooked.

Allow the soup to cool a little and remove the bay leaf. Using a blender or food processor, purée the soup in batches until smooth. Add a little more stock, if necessary, to achieve the required consistency. Return the soup to the hob and heat through gently, without boiling. Check the seasoning and serve.

Cream of mushroom soup

Porcini mushrooms give this homemade soup a depth of flavour that surpasses the dehydrated packet or canned types of soup.

Serves 4
Preparation time: 25 minutes + 30 minutes soaking
Cooking time: 15 minutes

15 g (½ oz) dried **porcini mushrooms**
1 tablespoon **olive oil**
1 large **onion**, finely chopped
225 g (8 oz) **flat mushrooms**, halved and sliced
1 **garlic clove**, crushed
850 ml (1½ pints) **vegetable stock**
salt and freshly ground **black pepper**

To garnish
4 tablespoons **crème fraîche**
chopped fresh **parsley**

Place the porcini mushrooms in a small bowl. Pour over 150 ml (5 fl oz) of warm water and leave to soak for 30 minutes.

Heat the oil in a large lidded saucepan and sauté the onion for 10 minutes, until softened. Add the soaked mushrooms with their soaking liquid, the flat mushrooms, garlic, stock and seasoning. Bring to the boil, reduce the heat, cover and simmer for 15 minutes.

Allow the soup to cool a little and reserve a few of the mushrooms. Using a blender or food processor, purée the remaining soup in batches until smooth. Return the soup to the hob and heat through gently, without boiling.

Pour into individual serving bowls. Place a tablespoon of crème fraîche in the middle of each serving, add a couple of mushroom slices and sprinkle with a little chopped parsley.

Seriously spicy lentil soup

A wonderfully robust soup based on a traditional Indian dhal. Adjust the quantity of chilli according to your own taste.

Serves 6
Preparation and
cooking time:
45 minutes

1 tablespoon **vegetable oil**
1 **onion**, chopped
1 **red pepper**, de-seeded
and diced
2 **garlic cloves**, crushed
2.5 cm (1 inch) **fresh root**
ginger, finely chopped
½ teaspoon **chilli powder**
½ teaspoon **turmeric**
½ teaspoon **ground**
coriander
225 g (8 oz) **split red lentils**
850 ml (1½ pints) **vegetable**
stock, plus extra if
needed
400 g can **chopped**
tomatoes
1 tablespoon **tomato purée**
salt and freshly ground
black pepper

To garnish
natural **yogurt**
finely chopped fresh
coriander leaves

Heat the vegetable oil in a large lidded saucepan and gently fry the onion for 3–4 minutes until softened but not coloured. Stir in the pepper and garlic and cook for a further 3–4 minutes.

Add the ginger, chilli powder, turmeric, ground coriander and lentils. Stir well to coat with the oil. Add the vegetable stock, tomatoes and tomato purée, stir and bring up to the boil. Reduce the heat, cover the pan and simmer the soup for 20–25 minutes, stirring occasionally, until the lentils are cooked.

Using a blender or food processor, blend half the soup to give a chunky texture. If you prefer a smoother textured soup, then purée the whole amount. Reheat the soup, adjusting the seasoning to taste and topping up with extra stock if needed to adjust the thickness of the soup. Ladle into warmed bowls and garnish with a swirl of yogurt and chopped coriander.

Tip For an optional garnish, heat 1 tablespoon of sunflower oil in a small non-stick frying pan and fry 1 teaspoon of crushed coriander seeds and ¼ teaspoon of turmeric until golden.

Pea & mint soup

This soup has a wonderful flavour and colour even though it uses frozen peas. Of course, you can use peas and mint fresh from the garden.

Serves 4
Preparation time: 25 minutes
Cooking time: 20 minutes

a bunch of **spring onions**, chopped
1 **potato**, peeled and diced
2 tablespoons chopped **fresh mint**, plus 7 extra sprigs
850 ml (1½ pints) **vegetable stock**
500 g (1 lb 2 oz) frozen **garden peas**
200 ml (7 fl oz) **crème fraîche**
freshly ground **black pepper** (optional)

Place the spring onions, potato and 3 whole mint sprigs in a large lidded saucepan. Pour over the vegetable stock and bring up to the boil. Reduce the heat, cover and simmer gently for 15 minutes until the potato is tender.

Add the peas, bring back to simmering point and cook for a further 5 minutes until the peas are tender. Remove the pan from the heat and discard the mint sprigs.

Allow the soup to cool a little and then mash for a chunky texture or, using a blender or food processor, purée the soup in batches until smooth. Return the soup to the pan and stir in the crème fraîche and chopped mint. Reheat the soup gently, but do not allow to boil. Check the seasoning and add a little freshly ground black pepper if required.

Serve the soup in warmed bowls and garnish each with a small sprig of fresh mint.

Golden broth

A traditional soup from Northern Ireland thickened with oatmeal and full of delicious vegetables. Serve with some freshly baked wholemeal soda bread.

Serves 4
Preparation time: 20 minutes
Cooking time: 40-45 minutes

25 g (1 oz) **butter**
1 large **onion**, finely chopped
1 **celery stick**, finely chopped
2 **carrots**, peeled and finely chopped
25 g (1 oz) **plain flour**
600 ml (20 fl oz) **chicken stock**, plus extra if needed
300 ml (10 fl oz) **semi-skimmed milk**
25 g (1 oz) medium **oatmeal**
125 g (4½ oz) **spinach**, washed and chopped
freshly ground **black pepper**

Melt the butter in a large lidded saucepan. Add the onion, celery and carrots and cook for 4–5 minutes to just soften the vegetables.

Stir in the flour and cook for a further minute, stirring constantly. Pour in the chicken stock followed by the milk and bring to the boil, stirring, to thicken the soup slightly. Reduce the heat, cover the pan and simmer gently for 30 minutes. Stir occasionally.

Sprinkle the oatmeal over the surface of the soup and stir it in. Add the spinach and stir that in. If necessary, add a little extra stock to reduce the thickness of the soup. Continue to cook gently for a further 10–15 minutes, stirring occasionally to prevent the soup sticking.

Serve the soup immediately in warmed bowls, garnished with a grinding of black pepper.

Tip Don't worry if it looks as if you have too much spinach to fit into the pan, it wilts down very quickly as soon as it touches the liquid.

Carrot & parsnip soup

The distinctive flavours of carrot and parsnip combine well to make this colourful and warming soup.

Serves 4
Preparation time: 15 minutes
Cooking time: 20 minutes

300 g (10½ oz) **parsnips**, peeled and chopped
300 g (10½ oz) **carrots**, peeled and chopped
1 **onion**, chopped
600 ml (20 fl oz) good **chicken** or **vegetable stock**
¼–½ teaspoon freshly grated **nutmeg**
freshly ground **black pepper**
chopped fresh **parsley**, to garnish

Place all the vegetables in a large lidded saucepan and pour half the stock over them. Cover with a lid, bring to the boil and then simmer until tender.

Add the remaining stock. Allow the soup to cool a little and then, using a blender or food processor, purée the soup in batches until smooth.

Return the soup to the hob and reheat gently. Season to taste with nutmeg and black pepper and serve garnished with the fresh parsley.

Butternut squash soup

An unusual soup, which is really easy to make. To vary the flavour, add a tablespoon of chopped fresh herbs in place of the nutmeg.

Serves 4
Preparation time: 20 minutes
Cooking time: 20-30 minutes

1 **butternut squash**, peeled, de-seeded and diced
2 **onions**, chopped
1 large **leek**, chopped
2 large **celery sticks**, chopped
425 ml (15 fl oz) **vegetable stock**
½ teaspoon freshly grated **nutmeg**
freshly ground **black pepper**

Put all the vegetables into a large lidded saucepan with 300 ml (10 fl oz) of the stock. Cover, bring to the boil and then simmer for 20–30 minutes, until all the vegetables are tender.

Add the remaining stock. Allow the soup to cool a little and then, using a blender or food processor, purée the soup in batches until smooth.

Return the soup to the hob and reheat gently. Season to taste with nutmeg and black pepper and serve immediately.

Italian bean soup

There's a real flavour of the Mediterranean in this filling soup. You could serve it as a main course accompanied by a tomato and olive bread.

Serves 6
Preparation time: 30 minutes
Cooking time: 30 minutes

2 tablespoons **olive oil**
50 g (1¾ oz) **pancetta**, cubed
1 **onion**, chopped
1 **celery stick**, diced
1 **carrot**, peeled and diced
1 **garlic clove**, crushed
½ teaspoon dried **sage**
1 **bay leaf**
400 g can **chopped tomatoes**
1 litre (1¾ pints) **vegetable stock**
400 g can **borlotti beans**, drained and rinsed
400 g can **cannellini beans**, drained and rinsed
100 g (3½ oz) **French beans**, cut into 4 cm (1½ inch) lengths
75 g (2¾ oz) **spaghetti**, broken into short pieces
1 tablespoon chopped fresh **parsley**
freshly ground **black pepper**

Heat the olive oil in a large lidded saucepan. Add the pancetta and fry gently for 2–3 minutes. Stir in the onion, celery, carrot, garlic, sage and bay leaf. Cook gently for a further 4–5 minutes to soften the vegetables.

Stir in the tomatoes and stock. Bring up to the boil, reduce the heat, cover and simmer gently for 15 minutes. Add the borlotti and cannellini beans and simmer for a further 5 minutes. Remove the bay leaf.

Ladle half the soup into a blender or food processor and purée until smooth. Return to the pan containing the remaining soup and add the French beans and spaghetti pieces. Cook for 7–8 minutes until the spaghetti is 'al dente' and the French beans are just tender.

Remove from the heat and stir in the parsley. Season to taste with black pepper if required. Serve immediately.

Sweet potato & onion soup

This velvety smooth soup was inspired by an old Norfolk recipe. The tangy onions complement the rich creaminess of the sweet potatoes.

Serves 4
Preparation time: 15 minutes
Cooking time: 20 minutes

1 tablespoon **olive oil**
2 large **onions**, sliced
500 g (1 lb 2 oz) **sweet potatoes**, peeled and roughly chopped
850 ml (1½ pints) **chicken** or **vegetable stock**
freshly ground **black pepper**

Heat half the oil in a large lidded saucepan and add half the onions. Fry gently until golden and crispy and then remove with a slotted spoon and reserve.

Add the remaining oil and onions to the pan and fry gently until softened. Add the sweet potatoes and half the stock. Bring to the boil, cover and simmer until the vegetables are tender.

Allow the soup to cool a little and then add the remaining stock. Using a blender or food processor, purée the soup in batches until smooth.

Return the soup to the hob and reheat gently. Season to taste with black pepper and serve garnished with the reserved onions and a grinding of black pepper.

Hearty turkey soup

A clever way to use up leftover turkey at Christmas, this soup is great at any time of the year and can also be made using cooked chicken.

Serves 4–6
Preparation time: 35 minutes
Cooking time: 30 minutes

1 tablespoon **sunflower oil**
1 large **onion**, chopped
3 **celery sticks**, chopped
450 g (1 lb) **potatoes**, peeled and diced
675 g (1½ lb) mixed **root vegetables** (e.g. carrot, parsnip, swede or turnip), peeled and diced
1.1 litres (2 pints) **chicken** or **turkey stock**
400 g can **haricot beans**, drained and rinsed
225 g (8 oz) **cooked turkey**, shredded
2–3 tablespoons chopped fresh **parsley**
salt and freshly ground **black pepper**

Heat the oil in a large saucepan and cook the onion until soft. Stir in the celery, potatoes and root vegetables and cook for 5 minutes.

Add the stock and haricot beans, bring to the boil and simmer for 25 minutes or until the vegetables are soft.

Stir in the turkey and parsley and heat through for 5 minutes. Season to taste before serving.

Main
meals

Thai chicken curry

If you can, use galangal and kaffir lime leaves for a truly authentic curry. Serve with steamed jasmine rice and lime wedges to squeeze over.

Serves 4
Preparation and
** cooking time:**
** 25 minutes**

1 **lemongrass stem**
450 g (1 lb) skinless,
   boneless **chicken breasts**
1 tablespoon **vegetable oil**
1 **red chilli**, de-seeded and
   finely chopped
1 teaspoon grated fresh **root**
   ginger or **galangal**
1 **garlic clove**, crushed
225 g (8 oz) **chestnut**, **oyster**
   or **shiitake mushrooms**,
   stalks removed, halved
a bunch of **spring onions**,
   sliced thinly, 1 reserved
   for garnish
300 ml (10 fl oz) **coconut**
   milk
150 ml (5 fl oz) **chicken stock**
zest of ½ a **lime**, pared in
   thick strips, plus extra
   thin strips to garnish, or
   2 **kaffir lime leaves**
1 rounded tablespoon
   chopped fresh **coriander**
1 tablespoon **soy sauce**

Remove any tough outer leaves from the lemongrass. Cut the stem into three and bruise the pieces. Cut the chicken breasts into bite-sized pieces, about eight each.

Heat the oil in a wok or large frying pan. Add the lemongrass, chicken, chilli, ginger or galangal and garlic. Stir fry for 2 minutes to seal the meat. Stir in the mushrooms and cook for a further minute.

Add the spring onions, coconut milk, stock, lime zest or lime leaves, coriander and soy sauce. Bring to the boil, reduce the heat and simmer gently for 8 minutes or until the chicken pieces are cooked.

Remove the lemongrass and lime zest or leaves. Shred the remaining spring onion and scatter it over to garnish, together with thin strips of lime zest.

Chicken with beans

A quick recipe suitable for a midweek evening meal – it only needs to be accompanied by boiled new potatoes and some lightly steamed broccoli.

Serves 4
Preparation time: 15 minutes
Cooking time: 30-35 minutes

1 **onion**, chopped
4 rashers **smoked back bacon**, chopped
1 **garlic clove**, chopped
4 skinless, boneless **chicken breasts**, cubed
400 g can **chopped tomatoes**
1 teaspoon dried **thyme**
1 teaspoon **paprika**
410 g can **cannellini beans**, drained and rinsed
freshly ground **black pepper**
chopped fresh **parsley**, to garnish

Gently fry the onion, bacon and garlic in a large, lidded, non stick pan for 5–6 minutes to soften the onion and cook the bacon. Add the chicken and continue to cook until the chicken is sealed and lightly golden.

Stir in the tomatoes along with the thyme and paprika. Bring up to the boil and then cover and reduce the heat. Simmer for 20–25 minutes, stirring occasionally.

Add the cannellini beans to the pan and stir into the mixture. Cook for a further 10 minutes until the beans are heated through and the chicken cooked. Season to taste with freshly ground black pepper. Serve immediately, sprinkled with some chopped parsley.

Tip Although the excess fat should be removed from the bacon, there should still be sufficient rendered out in the heat of the pan to cook off the onion and garlic – so don't be tempted to add any oil.

Chinese-style chicken

The secret of a good stir fry is having all of the ingredients prepared beforehand. Serve with steamed jasmine or basmati rice.

Serves 4
Preparation time: 15
minutes
Cooking time:
10 minutes

2 skinless, boneless
chicken breasts, sliced
into thin strips
2 teaspoons **Chinese five**
spice
1 tablespoon **sesame oil**
1 **garlic clove**, finely sliced
a walnut-sized piece of
fresh **root ginger**, cut into
matchsticks
a bunch of **spring onions**,
sliced diagonally
100 g (3½ oz) **mangetout**,
halved
1 **green pepper**, halved,
de-seeded and finely
sliced
a good shake of light **soy**
sauce

Toss the chicken strips in the Chinese five spice.

Heat the oil in a non stick wok or pan, add the garlic and ginger and quickly fry until just golden. Add the chicken and fry for 3–4 minutes.

Remove the chicken, garlic and ginger and keep warm. Add all the prepared vegetables to the wok together with 3 tablespoons of water.

Stir fry over a high heat for 2 minutes until the water has evaporated. Return the chicken, garlic and ginger to the pan. Add the soy sauce and toss to mix well. Serve immediately.

Chicken with black pudding

A Scottish version of the favourite English lamb or beef hotpot. To spice up the sauce, finely diced black pudding has been added. Serve with peas.

Serves 4
Preparation time:
 25 minutes
Cooking time:
 1¾ hours

1 tablespoon **sunflower oil**
2 **onions**, thinly sliced
2 tablespoons **plain flour**
salt and freshly ground
 black pepper
8 boneless, skinless
 chicken thighs
40 g (1½ oz) unsalted **butter**
900 g (2 lb) **potatoes**, thinly
 sliced
1 **dessert apple**, cored
 and sliced
110 g (4 oz) **black pudding**,
 diced
450 ml (16 fl oz) **chicken**
 stock

Preheat the oven to 180°C/350°F/Gas Mark 4. Heat the oil in the base of a lidded flameproof and ovenproof casserole dish, add the onions and fry for 5 minutes, stirring until softened. Remove with a slotted spoon and set aside.

Sift the flour into a shallow dish and season. Use to coat the chicken thighs. Melt half the butter in the casserole dish and fry the chicken in batches until golden on both sides. Remove from the dish and reserve with the onions.

Arrange half the potatoes in the base of the dish, top with the chicken, onions, apple and black pudding and then add the remaining potatoes, arranged overlapping on top. Pour over the stock, season and bring to the boil.

Cover with a lid and transfer to the oven for 1¼ hours. Remove the lid, dot with the remaining butter and cook for a further 30 minutes, uncovered, until the potatoes are golden. Spoon into shallow bowls to serve.

Chicken pasta bake

Serves 4
Preparation time:
20 minutes
Cooking time:
1 hour 20 minutes–
1 hour 30 minutes

1 tablespoon **olive oil**
500 g (1lb 2 oz) boneless,
    skinless **chicken thighs**,
    cubed
1 **onion**, chopped
1 **red pepper**, de-seeded
    and diced
1 **orange pepper**, de-seeded
    and diced
2 **garlic cloves**, finely
    chopped
1 tablespoon **cornflour**
400 g can **chopped**
    tomatoes
300 ml (10 fl oz) **chicken**
    stock
3 fresh **rosemary sprigs**,
    leaves chopped
salt and freshly ground
    black pepper
500 g (1 lb 2 oz) fresh **pasta**
    quills
a kettle full of **boiling water**
100 g (3 ½ oz) **mascarpone**
    cheese
80 g (3 oz) **Parmesan**
    cheese, grated

Preheat the oven to 180°C/350°F/Gas Mark 4. Heat the oil in a flameproof and ovenproof casserole dish, add the chicken a few pieces at a time, until all the pieces are in the dish, and then fry for 5 minutes, stirring until evenly browned. Remove with a slotted spoon and set aside on a plate.

Add the onion to the dish and fry for 5 minutes until softened and just beginning to turn golden. Add the peppers and garlic and cook for a few minutes until just beginning to soften.

Mix the cornflour with a little water until a smooth paste forms and then add to the dish with the tomatoes, stock and rosemary. Season, bring to the boil, stirring, and then add the chicken pieces back in. Cover and transfer to the oven to cook for 1 hour.

When the chicken is almost ready, tip the pasta into a large bowl, cover with boiling water and leave to soak for 5 minutes. Drain.

Remove the casserole dish from the oven, stir the mascarpone into the hot chicken mix and then gently fold in the pasta. Sprinkle with the Parmesan and return the dish to the oven, uncovered, for 20–30 minutes until golden.

Chicken in Dijon sauce

This is a simple all-in-one meal that can be prepared in advance and then cooked just before serving. Serve with rice or baked potatoes.

Serves 4
Preparation time:
  20 minutes + 1 hour
  marinating
Cooking time:
  30–40 minutes

4 boneless, skinless
  chicken breasts
300 ml (10 fl oz) **white wine**
2 tablespoons **Dijon**
  mustard
3 tablespoons **olive oil**
2 **courgettes**, sliced
4 small **carrots**, peeled
  and diced
115 g (4¼ oz) **button**
  mushrooms
2 tablespoons **cornflour**
300 ml (10 fl oz) **chicken**
  stock

Cut each chicken breast into six slices and place in a shallow dish. Mix together the white wine and Dijon mustard and pour over the chicken. Leave to marinate, covered, in the fridge for at least 1 hour. Preheat the oven to 180°C/350°F/Gas Mark 4.

Heat the oil in a lidded flameproof and ovenproof casserole dish. Remove the chicken from the marinade, add to the casserole dish and brown on all sides (reserve the marinade). Add the courgettes, carrots and mushrooms and cook for 5 minutes.

Mix the cornflour with a little of the stock and add to the dish with the remaining stock and the marinade. Heat gently until the sauce has thickened.

Cover, transfer to the oven and cook for 30–40 minutes until the chicken is cooked right through.

Chicken korma

For the best flavour the chicken is best left to marinate overnight in yogurt, turmeric and garlic. Serve with rice mixed with chopped fresh coriander.

Serves 4
Preparation time:
  20 minutes +
  overnight marinating
Cooking time:
  30 minutes

4 boneless, skinless
  chicken breasts
150 g (5½ oz) natural **yogurt**
2 **garlic cloves**, crushed
2 teaspoons **turmeric**
40 g (1½ oz) unsalted **butter**
1 large **onion**, sliced
5 cm (2 inches) fresh **root**
  ginger, finely diced
1 teaspoon **chilli powder**
1 teaspoon **coriander**
  seeds, crushed
10 whole **cloves**
1 teaspoon **salt**
5 cm (2 inch) **cinnamon**
  stick
1 tablespoon **cornflour**
150 ml (5 fl oz) **single cream**
25 g (1 oz) **unsalted cashew**
  nuts, toasted, to garnish

Score each chicken breast with a sharp knife. In a large bowl, mix together the yogurt, garlic and turmeric. Add the chicken and coat well in the marinade. Cover and leave to marinate overnight in the fridge.

Melt the butter in a large frying pan, add the onion and cook until soft and browned. Stir in the ginger, chilli powder, coriander seeds, cloves, salt and cinnamon stick and cook for 2–3 minutes.

Add the chicken and its marinade and cook on a gentle heat for 20–25 minutes until the chicken is completely cooked. Reduce the heat.

Blend the cornflour and cream together and stir into the chicken. Reheat very gently to prevent the cream from curdling. Sprinkle over the cashew nuts to garnish and serve.

Pot-roast pesto chicken

Sunday lunch needn't mean lots of pans on the hob. Add everything to one pan then cover and roast in the oven – what could be simpler?

Serves 4
Preparation time:
  20 minutes
Cooking time:
  1 hour 55 minutes

1.5 kg (3 lb 2 oz) whole
  chicken
2 **red** or **white onions**,
  cut into wedges
450 g (1 lb) **tomatoes**,
  roughly chopped
6 **garlic cloves**, finely
  chopped
3 tablespoons **pesto**
1 teaspoon **paprika**
salt and freshly ground
  black pepper
600 ml (10 fl oz) hot **chicken
  stock**
550 g (1 lb 3 oz) **butternut
  squash**, peeled, de-seeded
  and cut into wedges
300 g (10½ oz) **courgettes**,
  thickly sliced
1 **red pepper**, de-seeded
  and thickly sliced
1 **yellow pepper**, de-seeded
  and thickly sliced

Preheat the oven to 180°C/350°F/Gas Mark 4. Add the chicken to a large, lidded, flameproof and ovenproof casserole dish or oval covered roaster. Tuck the onions, tomatoes and garlic around the chicken. Spread 2 tablespoons of pesto over the chicken and then sprinkle with the paprika and season. Pour the stock around the chicken. Cover and transfer to the oven to cook for 1¼ hours.

Remove the lid, baste the chicken breast with the stock and then add the remaining vegetables, pressing as many as you can beneath the stock. Cook, uncovered, for 30 minutes.

Remove from the oven, turn the vegetables, baste with the stock and then spread the remaining 1 tablespoon of pesto over the chicken breasts. Cook for 10 more minutes or until the chicken and vegetables are cooked through and the chicken is golden brown.

Lift out the chicken, carve and serve in shallow bowls with the vegetables and the stock ladled over.

Tarragon chicken

Fresh tarragon has a wonderful aniseed flavour, but don't ever use dried tarragon – it tastes dreadful. Serve with new potatoes and a green salad.

Serves 4
Preparation time:
 35 minutes
Cooking time:
 45 minutes

8 skinless **chicken thighs**
125 ml (4 fl oz) **dry white wine**
½ **onion**, finely sliced
25 g (1 oz) fresh **tarragon**, leaves separated from stalks
1 **chicken stock cube**
salt and freshly ground **black pepper**
100 g (3½ oz) **crème fraîche**

Preheat the oven to 190°C/375°F/Gas Mark 5. Put the chicken in a lidded flameproof casserole dish, add the wine, onion, half the tarragon leaves and the tarragon stalks and 125 ml (4 fl oz) of water. Crumble over the stock cube and season.

Cover and cook in the oven for 45 minutes until the chicken is cooked through. Remove the chicken thighs and keep warm.

Boil the stock over a high heat until reduced by half and then remove the tarragon stalks.

Add the crème fraîche (don't worry if it looks curdled) and boil, stirring well until the sauce thickens. Chop the remaining tarragon leaves, add to the dish and check the seasoning. Put the chicken back into the sauce, stir well and serve.

Braised pork with fennel

A simple pork casserole made with just six ingredients, but full of flavour. The fennel adds sweetness. Serve with roasted sweet potatoes.

Serves 4
Preparation time:
 25 minutes
Cooking time:
 25–30 minutes

2 tablespoons **sunflower oil**
4 x 175–225 g (6–8 oz) **pork steaks**
225 g (8 oz) **fennel bulb**
1 **red pepper**, de-seeded and diced
225 g (8 oz) **mushrooms**, quartered
400 g can **chopped tomatoes**
salt and freshly ground **black pepper**

Preheat the oven to 200°C/400°F/Gas Mark 6. Heat the oil in a lidded flameproof and ovenproof casserole dish and brown the pork steaks on both sides. Remove and set aside.

Thinly slice the fennel and reserve any feathery leaves for garnish. Cook the fennel slices in the casserole dish until softened. Remove and set aside with the pork steaks.

Fry the pepper and mushrooms for about 5 minutes until soft and then stir in the tomatoes and bring to the boil. Season. Return the pork steaks and fennel to the casserole dish, making sure the steaks are covered by the sauce. Cover with the lid.

Cook for 25–30 minutes until the pork is cooked through and the vegetables are tender. Serve garnished with the feathery fennel leaves.

Pork with herby dumplings

This warming casserole is served with light herby dumplings, which are cooked on the top of the dish and absorb lots of the wonderful flavours.

Serves 4
Preparation time: 30 minutes
Cooking time: 1 hour 20 minutes

1 tablespoon **olive oil**
675 g (1½ lb) lean boneless **pork**, cubed
1 **onion**, sliced
2 tablespoons **plain flour**
1 litre (1¾ pints) **dry cider**
2 **carrots**, peeled and chopped
2 **eating apples**, cored and sliced
1 **bouquet garni**
2 tablespoons **Dijon mustard**
2 tablespoons **Worcestershire sauce**
salt and freshly ground **black pepper**

Herby dumplings
115 g (4¼ oz) **self-raising flour**
50 g (1¾ oz) **vegetable suet**
2 tablespoons chopped fresh or 1 teaspoon dried **mixed herbs**

Preheat the oven to 180°C/350°F/Gas Mark 4. Heat the oil in a large, lidded, flameproof and ovenproof casserole dish and fry the pork until browned. Remove with a slotted spoon and set aside. Add the onion and fry for 5 minutes until lightly browned. Stir in the flour and cook for 1 minute and then gradually stir in the cider until smooth.

Return the pork to the pan with the carrots, apples, bouquet garni, Dijon mustard and Worcestershire sauce. Season well. Cover and cook in the oven for 1 hour.

Meanwhile, mix the flour, suet, herbs and seasoning together. Add 3–4 tablespoons of water and mix lightly to a soft dough. Shape into eight balls. Remove the casserole dish from the oven and add the dumplings, spaced slightly apart. Cover and cook for a further 20 minutes until the dumplings are risen and light.

Sweet & sour pork

Making your own sweet and sour sauce is straightforward, delicious, and infinitely preferable to the ready-made alternative.

Serves 4
Preparation time: 10 minutes
Cooking time: 15 minutes

2 tablespoons **sunflower oil**
350 g (12 oz) **pork fillet** or **tenderloin**, sliced into 1 cm (½ inch) medallions, then halved
1 **onion**, roughly chopped
½ **red pepper,** de-seeded and chopped
½ **green pepper**, de-seeded and chopped
225 g can **bamboo shoots**, drained and rinsed
1½ tablespoons **cornflour**

Sauce
3 tablespoons **cider vinegar**
3 tablespoons **soft light brown sugar**
2 tablespoons **soy sauce**
1½ tablespoons **tomato purée**
150 ml (5 fl oz) **pineapple juice**

For the sauce, combine the vinegar, sugar, soy sauce and tomato purée in a small bowl. Make the pineapple juice up to 225 ml (8 fl oz) with water and stir into the mixture.

Heat 1 tablespoon of the oil in a large lidded wok or frying pan. Add the pork and stir fry over a high heat for 1–2 minutes, turning the meat continuously, until browned. Remove from the pan and set aside.

Add the remaining oil to the pan. Stir fry the onion and peppers for 1 minute. Return the pork to the pan and add the sauce and bamboo shoots. Bring to the boil, reduce the heat, cover and simmer for 5 minutes.

Blend the cornflour with 2 tablespoons of water. Remove the lid from the wok or pan, stir in the cornflour mixture and bubble until the mixture thickens. Heat through, stirring all the time, for 1 minute. Serve at once.

Variation Substitute chicken for the pork, if you prefer.

Madeira pork

A creamy sauce flavoured with Madeira and mushrooms – simple but delicious. Serve with carrot and potato mash and your favourite vegetables.

Serves 4
Preparation time: 25 minutes
Cooking time: 20 minutes

2–3 tablespoons **sunflower oil**
1 **onion**, chopped
1 large **yellow pepper**, de-seeded and diced
675 g (1½ lb) **pork fillet**, trimmed of visible fat and cut into 1 cm (½ inch) slices
1 tablespoon **paprika**
1 tablespoon **plain flour**
300 ml (10 fl oz) **stock**
150 ml (5 fl oz) **Madeira**
175 g (6 oz) **button mushrooms**, quartered
1 tablespoon **tomato purée**
salt and freshly ground **black pepper**
150 ml (5 fl oz) **single cream**

Heat the oil in a large lidded frying pan. Add the onion and pepper and cook for 3–4 minutes. Add the pork slices and brown on all sides. Stir in the paprika and flour and cook for 1 minute.

Blend in the stock and Madeira, bring to the boil and reduce the heat to a simmer. Stir in the mushrooms and tomato purée and season. Cover the pan and simmer gently for 20 minutes or until the pork is tender and cooked through.

Stir in the cream, heat gently and serve straight away.

Variation Ruby port can be used in place of the Madeira if you prefer.

Boiled gammon & peas

Soaked yellow split peas are tied in a cloth and simmered in the same pan as a gammon joint for a nostalgic supper. Serve with English mustard.

Serves 4
Preparation time:
  25 minutes +
  overnight soaking
Cooking time:
  1 hour 50 minutes

1.25 kg (2 lb 12 oz) smoked
  gammon joint
250 g (9 oz) dried **yellow
  split peas**
2 **onions**, quartered
2 **bay leaves**
350 g (12 oz) **carrots**, peeled
  and cut into large chunks
225 g (8 oz) **turnips**, peeled
  and quartered or halved
4 **celery sticks**, thickly sliced
5 **cloves**
a few **black peppercorns**,
  roughly crushed
350 g (12 oz) **potatoes**, peeled
  and cut into chunks
2 **small leeks**, cut into 2.5 cm
  (1 inch) lengths
40 g (1½ oz) unsalted **butter**
salt and freshly ground **black
  pepper**
chopped fresh **parsley**,
  to garnish

Add the gammon joint and split peas to separate bowls and cover each with cold water. Leave the peas at room temperature but transfer the gammon to the fridge overnight.

The next day, drain the gammon and split peas. Add the gammon, 1 onion, the bay leaves, carrots, turnip, celery, cloves and peppercorns to a large lidded saucepan. Tie the drained split peas, remaining onion and the potatoes in a large piece of muslin or a linen tea cloth. Add to the pan, cover with cold water and bring to the boil.

Boil rapidly for 10 minutes, skimming any froth off the surface if needed. Reduce the heat to a simmer, cover and cook for 1½ hours or until the gammon and split peas are tender. Add the leeks and cook for a further 10 minutes until just tender.

Lift the bag of split peas from the pan, untie the string and tip the peas, potato and onion into a large bowl. Mash with the butter, a little extra pepper and salt to taste. Spoon onto serving plates.

Carve the gammon and add to the plates with the cooked vegetables, some of the broth and a sprinkling of chopped parsley.

Dijonnaise pork

This is based on a wonderful French recipe. Don't be tempted to use English mustard – it's far too fiery and would completely spoil the sauce.

Serves 4
Preparation time: 15 minutes
Cooking time: 20 minutes

1 tablespoon **sunflower oil**
4 large **pork loin chops**, trimmed of visible fat
freshly ground **black pepper**
100 ml (3½ fl oz) **dry white wine**
1 teaspoon dried **thyme**
150 g (5½ oz) **crème fraîche**
1 teaspoon **tomato purée**
1 tablespoon **Dijon mustard**
1 **tomato**, peeled, de-seeded and diced
1 tablespoon chopped fresh **parsley**

Heat the oil in a large frying pan. Season the pork chops with black pepper and add to the pan. Seal quickly on both sides and then reduce the heat. Cook the chops for a further 3 minutes on each side then remove from the pan to a plate. Pour off all the excess fat and wipe out the pan with kitchen towel.

Return the pan to the heat and pour in the wine. Add the thyme and bubble vigorously for 2–3 minutes until the wine is reduced to about one third of its original volume.

Stir in the crème fraîche and tomato purée and then return the pork chops to the pan. Cook the chops for 5–6 minutes over a medium heat until tender, being careful not to overcook them.

Stir in the Dijon mustard, tomato and chopped parsley. Continue to cook for a further 2–3 minutes until heated through. Serve the chops immediately, with the sauce.

Pork & plum casserole

Best cooked in the late summer, do make sure the plums are ripe. Serve with mashed potatoes and green vegetables.

Serves 6
Preparation time:
   35 minutes
Cooking time:
   1½ hours

1 teaspoon **vegetable oil**
1½ teaspoons **Chinese five spice**
1 **red onion**, sliced
1 **onion**, sliced
2 **garlic cloves**, sliced
3 **celery sticks**, sliced
2 teaspoons dried **basil**
675 g (1½ lb) **lean pork**, cubed
300 ml (10 fl oz) **red wine**
450 g (1 lb) ripe **red plums**, quartered and stoned
1 tablespoon **cornflour**
salt and freshly ground **black pepper**
chopped fresh **parsley**, to garnish (optional)

Preheat the oven to 160°C/320°F/Gas Mark 3. Heat the oil in a lidded flameproof and ovenproof casserole dish. Add the Chinese five spice and cook over a gentle heat for 30 seconds. Add both onions and the garlic and stir fry for 2 minutes. Add the celery and stir fry for 1 minute.

Sprinkle on the basil and stir in the pork and wine, with three-quarters of the plums. Bring to the boil, cover, place on a baking sheet and cook for about 1¼ hours, or until the pork is just tender.

Blend the cornflour to a smooth paste with a little cold water. Stir into the casserole, mixing it through all the liquid. Place the remaining plums on top and return to the oven for 15 minutes, or until the plums have heated through. Check the seasoning and garnish with the parsley, if using.

Tip If you prefer, the quantity of wine can be halved and stock used in its place.

Spicy beef stir fry

Always prepare the ingredients before starting to cook to ensure that cooking flows as rapidly as possible. Serve with cooked noodles or rice.

Serves 4
Preparation time: 20 minutes
Cooking time: 15 minutes

350 g (12 oz) lean **rump steak**, finely sliced

1½ teaspoons **Chinese five spice**

2 teaspoons **cornflour**

1 tablespoon **vegetable oil**

4 **spring onions**, sliced and halved if thick

1 **garlic clove**, finely chopped

1 **red chilli**, de-seeded and finely chopped

4 cm (1½ inches) fresh **root ginger**, finely chopped

1 **red pepper**, de-seeded and sliced

1 **green pepper**, de-seeded and sliced

125 g (4½ oz) **baby corn**, sliced on the diagonal

150 ml (5 fl oz) **beef stock**

3 tablespoons **oyster sauce**

freshly ground **black pepper**

Toss the rump steak with the Chinese five spice and cornflour to coat the meat. Set aside.

Heat the oil in a wok or large frying pan and stir fry the spring onions for 2 minutes. Add the garlic, chilli and ginger and fry for a further minute. Add the peppers and baby corn and stir fry until the vegetables are just tender – no more than 3–4 minutes. Transfer the vegetables to a plate and keep warm.

Add the beef to the wok and stir fry to brown completely. Pour in the stock and oyster sauce and cook for about 2 minutes until the stock thickens slightly. Season with black pepper.

Return the vegetables to the wok and stir fry for a further 2 minutes until everything is heated through. Take care not to overcook. Serve immediately.

Beef in Guinness cobbler

A traditional British stew with an American twist – the meat is topped with a layer of light scones. Serve with a selection of green vegetables.

Serves 4
Preparation time:
30 minutes
Cooking time:
1 hour 50 minutes–
2½ hours

50 g (1¾ oz) **plain flour**
½ teaspoon freshly grated
nutmeg
salt and freshly ground
black pepper
675 g (1½ lb) **chuck steak**,
cut into 2.5 cm (1 inch)
cubes
3 tablespoons **olive oil**
25 g (1 oz) unsalted **butter**
2 large **onions**, finely sliced
2 **garlic cloves**, crushed
1 teaspoon **brown sugar**
575 ml (19 fl oz) **Guinness**
zest and juice of an **orange**
1 **bay leaf**

Scone topping
225 g (8 oz) **self-raising flour**
a pinch of **salt**
50 g (1¾ oz) unsalted **butter**
7 tablespoons **semi-skimmed milk**

Preheat the oven to 180°C/350°F/Gas Mark 4. Sift the flour into a shallow dish and stir in the nutmeg and plenty of seasoning. Coat the meat in the flour.

Heat half the oil and half the butter in a large, lidded, flameproof and ovenproof casserole dish. Add half the meat and fry for 2–3 minutes until evenly browned. Transfer to a plate, add the remaining oil and butter to the casserole and brown the remaining meat. Transfer to the plate.

Put the onions and garlic in the casserole and fry gently for 5 minutes, stirring constantly. Add the sugar and cook over a moderate heat for a further minute, stirring constantly, until the sugar caramelises.

Return the beef to the casserole and pour the Guinness over the top. Add the orange zest and juice and bay leaf and bring to the boil.

Cover and cook for 1½–2 hours, stirring occasionally and adding a little water to the casserole if the liquid becomes too thick.

For the scone topping, sift the flour and salt into a large bowl and rub the butter in until the mixture forms fine breadcrumbs. Add enough milk to form a soft dough. Knead on a lightly floured surface, roll out to 1 cm (½ inch) thick and cut out 8 scones using a 5 cm (2 inch) cutter.

Remove the casserole from the oven, take off the lid and arrange the scones in an overlapping circle around the edge of the dish, with one in the centre. Return the dish, uncovered, to the oven and cook for a further 20–30 minutes or until the scones are well risen and golden brown.

Beef in red wine

This elegant casserole is great for a dinner party. Prepare the day before and keep in the fridge to let the flavours develop. Serve with garlic bread.

Serves 4
Preparation time:
  25 minutes
Cooking time:
  1½ hours

25 g (1 oz) **plain flour**
salt and freshly ground
  black pepper
500 g (1 lb 2 oz) lean
  braising steak, trimmed
  of visible fat and cubed
1 tablespoon **vegetable oil**
1 large **onion**, sliced
2 **garlic cloves**, crushed
2 **carrots**, peeled and sliced
2 **celery sticks**, sliced
300 ml (10 fl oz) **beef stock**
300 ml (10 fl oz) **red wine**
1 teaspoon dried **thyme**
2 **bay leaves**
2 tablespoons **tomato purée**
225 g (8 oz) **button
  mushrooms**, quartered

Preheat the oven to 160°C/320°F/Gas Mark 3. Sift the flour into a shallow dish and season well. Toss the beef in the seasoned flour to coat lightly.

Heat the oil in a large, lidded, flameproof and ovenproof casserole dish and fry off batches of the beef to brown and seal. Using a slotted spoon, transfer the beef to a plate.

Add the onion, garlic, carrots and celery to the casserole and cook gently for 5–6 minutes until softened. Pour in the beef stock and red wine and add the thyme, bay leaves and tomato purée. Stir to mix in the tomato purée and bring the mixture up to the boil.

Return the beef to the casserole dish, cover and cook in the oven for 1¼ hours. Remove the casserole from the oven, stir in the mushrooms and return to the oven for a further 15 minutes or until the beef is very tender. Check the seasoning and serve immediately.

Beef & sweet vegetables

In this recipe, onion is caramelised and several sweet vegetables are included to develop a sweeter flavour. Serve with baked potatoes.

Serves 4
Preparation time:
1 hour
Cooking time:
1 hour 35 minutes–
1 hour 50 minutes

1 **onion**, sliced
200 g (7 oz) **carrots**, peeled and chopped
200 g (7 oz) **leeks**, chopped
200 g (7 oz) **parsnips**, peeled and chopped
1 **sweet potato**, peeled and chopped
225 ml (8 fl oz) **beef stock**
225 ml (8 fl oz) **beer, ale** or **lager**
450 g (1 lb) **lean casserole beef pieces**, trimmed of visible fat
1 **bouquet garni**
freshly ground **black pepper**
2 level tablespoons **cornflour**

Put the onion in a large, lidded, flameproof and ovenproof casserole dish, cover with the lid and place over a low heat. Leave to become golden brown and slightly sticky. Check after 15 minutes to ensure the onion is beginning to brown; if not, raise the heat a little. When the onion is cooked and coloured, remove from the dish (this should take about 30 minutes in total). Preheat the oven to 160°C/320°F/Gas Mark 3.

Place all the other vegetables in the casserole dish. Pour over the stock and beer, ale or lager, cover and bring to the boil. Stir well. Add the beef and bouquet garni and season with black pepper. Stir in the reserved onion and cover.

Place on a baking tray and transfer to the oven. Cook for 1¼–1½ hours, or until the meat and vegetables are just tender.

Mix the cornflour to a smooth paste with a little cold water. Remove the casserole from the oven, pour the cornflour paste over and stir, taking care not to break up the vegetables. Replace the lid and return the casserole to the oven for another 20 minutes. Remove the bouquet garni and serve.

Tip Don't be tempted to cook the casserole for longer than the recommended time because really lean cuts of meat toughen very quickly, even in a casserole.

Lamb in mushroom sauce

Here lamb chops in a mushroom sauce are baked in the oven until tender.
Serve with brown rice and stir-fried courgettes and peppers.

Serves 4
Preparation time:
20 minutes
Cooking time:
1¼–1½ hours

40 g (1½ oz) unsalted **butter**
8 best end of neck **lamb
    chops**, trimmed of visible
    fat
1 tablespoon **plain flour**
300 ml (10 fl oz) **lamb stock**
4 tablespoons **redcurrant
    jelly**
2 tablespoons
    Worcestershire sauce
2 tablespoons freshly
    squeezed **lemon juice**
a pinch of freshly grated
    nutmeg
salt and freshly ground
    black pepper
225 g (8 oz) **button
    mushrooms**

Preheat the oven to 160°C/320°F/Gas Mark 3.
Melt the butter in a lidded flameproof and
ovenproof casserole dish and quickly brown
the chops on all sides. Remove to a plate.

Stir the flour into the remaining fat in the dish,
blend in the stock and add the redcurrant jelly,
Worcestershire sauce, lemon juice and
nutmeg. Season and heat until boiling,
stirring continuously.

Return the chops to the dish, together with
the mushrooms, making sure the sauce covers
the lamb. Cover and cook for 1¼–1½ hours or
until the chops are tender.

Mediterranean lamb

Reminiscent of Greek holidays – lamb is marinated in a spicy yogurt mixture and then simmered in a tomato sauce. Serve with a green salad.

Serves 4
**Preparation time: 20
  minutes + at least
  1 hour marinating**
**Cooking time:
  50–60 minutes**

225 g (8 oz) **Greek yogurt**
zest of a **lemon**
2 **garlic cloves**, crushed
1 teaspoon **ground cumin**
3 tablespoons **olive oil**
salt and freshly ground
  black pepper
675 g (1½ lb) **lamb fillet**,
  sliced
1 **onion**, thinly sliced
150 ml (5 fl oz) **dry white
  wine**
1 **lamb stock cube**
400 g can **chopped tomatoes**
1 tablespoon **tomato purée**
1 teaspoon **caster sugar**
2 **bay leaves**
1 tablespoon fresh **oregano**
80 g (3 oz) stoned **black
  olives**
175 g (6 oz) canned **artichoke
  hearts**
6 **mint leaves**, finely chopped

Spoon 3 tablespoons of the yogurt into a large bowl and stir in the lemon zest, garlic, ground cumin and 1 tablespoon of olive oil. Season, place the lamb in the marinade and stir to coat well. Place in the fridge for at least 1 hour to marinate.

Heat the remaining oil in a large lidded frying pan and fry the onion over a gentle heat until tender. Add the meat and fry until browned on all surfaces.

Pour the wine into the pan and stir well. crumble over the stock cube and then add the tomatoes, tomato purée, sugar, bay leaves and oregano. Cover the pan and simmer very gently for about 50–60 minutes until the meat is tender.

Stir in the olives and artichoke hearts and cook for 10 minutes. Mix the remaining Greek yogurt with the mint leaves and serve with the lamb.

Greek-style lamb shanks

This is cooked long and slow for meltingly tender lamb that almost falls off the bone. An easy dish to share with friends.

Serves 4
Preparation and cooking time: 3 hours

2 tablespoons **olive oil**
4 x 350 g (12 oz) **lamb shanks**
2 **onions**, roughly chopped
3 **garlic cloves**, finely chopped
2 teaspoons **coriander seeds**, roughly crushed
2 tablespoons **plain flour**
200 ml (7 fl oz) **white wine**
450 ml (16 fl oz) **lamb stock**, plus extra if needed
1 tablespoon thick-set or runny **honey**
1 **lemon**, cut into wedges
2 **bay leaves**
675 g (1½ lb) small **new potatoes**, scrubbed and thickly sliced
salt and freshly ground **black pepper**
80 g (3 oz) **mixed olives** and **sundried tomatoes**
150 g (5½ oz) frozen **green beans**
chopped **fresh parsley**, to garnish

Preheat the oven to 180°C/350°F/Gas Mark 4. Heat the oil in a large, lidded, flameproof and ovenproof casserole dish. Add the lamb, cooking in batches if needed, and fry, turning for about 5 minutes until brown all over. Remove and set aside.

Add the onions to the dish and fry for 5 minutes, stirring until just beginning to brown. Add the garlic and coriander seeds and then stir in the flour. Gradually pour in the wine and stock and bring to the boil. Add the honey, lemon and bay leaves and then the potato slices. Season.

Return the lamb to the dish, cover and transfer to the oven for 2¼ hours.

Remove the dish from the oven, turn the lamb and add the olives and sundried tomatoes and the still frozen beans. Top up with a little extra stock if needed, cover and cook for a further 15 minutes until the beans are hot and the lamb is very tender. Spoon into large shallow bowls and garnish with the chopped parsley.

Spicy meatball stew

A blend of hot and fiery chilli powder and mild and sweet paprika produces a hearty stew. Serve with spaghetti.

Serves 4
Preparation time: 15 minutes
Cooking time: 30 minutes

450 g (1 lb) **lamb mince**
115 g (4¼ oz) fresh **breadcrumbs**
1 **onion**, grated
1 tablespoon **paprika**
1 **garlic clove**, crushed
1 teaspoon **chilli powder**
25 g (1 oz) stoned **black olives**, chopped
1 tablespoon chopped fresh **parsley**, plus extra to garnish
1 **egg**, beaten
1 tablespoon **vegetable oil**
300 ml (10 fl oz) **lamb stock**
400 g can **chopped tomatoes**
2 **courgettes**, chopped
4 **bay leaves**
salt and freshly ground **black pepper**

In a large bowl, mix together the lamb, breadcrumbs, onion, paprika, garlic, chilli powder, olives, parsley and beaten egg. Ensure that the mixture is evenly combined and then shape into 16 even-sized small balls.

Heat the oil in a large frying pan and gently fry the meatballs for 5–10 minutes until they are evenly browned.

Add the stock, tomatoes, courgettes and bay leaves and season. Bring to the boil, reduce the heat to a gentle simmer, cover and cook for 30 minutes. Remove the bay leaves and serve garnished with extra parsley.

Lancashire hotpot

A traditional recipe of layers of lamb, sliced onions and potatoes cooked in a dish. Boiled carrots or mashed swede are ideal accompaniments.

Serves 4
Preparation time:
20 minutes
Cooking time:
1 hour 50 minutes–
2 hours 20 minutes

25 g (1 oz) **plain flour**
salt and freshly ground
   black pepper
675 g (1½ lb) middle or best
   end of neck **lamb chops,**
   trimmed of visible fat
2 large **onions**, sliced
2 **lamb's kidneys,** skinned,
   cored and sliced
675 g (1½ lb) **potatoes**,
   sliced
1 tablespoon chopped fresh
   rosemary
25 g (1 oz) unsalted **butter**,
   melted
425 ml (15 fl oz) **lamb stock**

Preheat the oven to 180°C/350°F/Gas Mark 4. Sift the flour into a shallow dish and season well. Add the chops and turn to coat evenly in the seasoned flour.

Arrange layers of meat, onion, kidney and potato in a large, lidded, ovenproof casserole dish. Sprinkle each layer with a little rosemary and some seasoning and finish with a layer of potatoes.

Brush the top of the potatoes with the melted butter. Pour the stock into the casserole dish and cover it tightly with a lid. Cook for 1½–2 hours, or until the meat is tender.

Remove the lid from the casserole and cook for an extra 20 minutes to brown the potatoes.

Tip If you don't have a lidded casserole dish, use a regular ovenproof dish and cover with foil.

Sausages & lamb's kidneys

A really meaty treat! Sausages and kidneys in a red wine sauce. Serve with creamy mashed potatoes and stir fried cabbage or greens.

Serves 4
Preparation time:
  20 minutes
Cooking time:
  40–50 minutes

25 g (1 oz) **plain flour**
salt and freshly ground
  black pepper
8 **lamb's kidneys**
450 g (1 lb) **sausages**
2 tablespoons **vegetable oil**
8 **button onions**, peeled
150 ml (5 fl oz) **beef stock**
150 ml (5 fl oz) **red wine**
2 tablespoons **tomato purée**
4 **bay leaves**

Sift the flour into a shallow dish and season well. Skin the kidneys and cut them in half. Snip out the central white core with scissors and discard, and then toss the kidneys in the seasoned flour. Separate the sausages and cut them in half.

Heat the oil in a large lidded frying pan and gently fry the onions until they are golden. Add the kidneys and sausages and fry until browned on all surfaces.

Stir in the stock, red wine, tomato purée and bay leaves. Bring to the boil and then reduce to a simmer. Cover and cook over a gentle heat for 40–50 minutes or until the sausages and kidneys are cooked. Check the seasoning and serve immediately.

Slow-cooked lamb

An easy, comforting winter supper. If you get a little delayed you may need to stir in some extra hot stock, as the barley keeps on absorbing the liquid.

Serves 4
Preparation time:
 30 minutes
Cooking time:
 2½ hours

1 tablespoon **sunflower oil**
500 g (1 lb 2 oz) **lamb fillet**, sliced
1 **onion**, chopped
225 g (8 oz) **swede**, peeled and diced
225 g (8 oz) **carrot**, peeled and diced
225 g (8 oz) **parsnip**, peeled and diced
150 g (5½ oz) **pearl barley**
1 litre (1¾ pints) **lamb stock**
3 fresh **rosemary sprigs**, plus extra chopped leaves to garnish
salt and freshly ground **black pepper**
chopped fresh **parsley**, to garnish

Preheat the oven to 170°C/325°F/Gas Mark 3. Heat the oil in a large, lidded, flameproof and ovenproof casserole dish, add the lamb a few pieces at a time and fry for 5 minutes until browned on both sides. Remove with a slotted spoon and set aside.

Add the onion and fry for 5 minutes, until softened and just beginning to brown. Mix in the root vegetables and toss together and then return the lamb to the dish. Add the pearl barley, stock and rosemary, season and bring to the boil.

Cover and transfer to the oven for 2½ hours until the lamb and vegetables are very tender.

Stir the casserole and serve in shallow bowls, sprinkled with parsley to garnish.

Salami & vegetable risotto

A classic Italian dish. Risotto rice has a wonderfully rich and creamy texture, quite unlike long grain rice.

Serves 4
Preparation time:
   20 minutes
Cooking time:
   35 minutes

3 tablespoons **olive oil**
2 **red onions**, sliced
1 **green pepper**, de-seeded
   and chopped
1 **red pepper**, de-seeded
   and chopped
115 g (4¼ oz) **button
   mushrooms**, halved
4 **tomatoes**, skinned and
   chopped
225 g (8 oz) **risotto rice**
850 ml (1½ pints) hot
   vegetable stock
225 g (8 oz) **salami**, cubed
salt and freshly ground
   black pepper
grated **Parmesan cheese**,
   to serve

Heat the oil in a deep frying pan, add the onions and cook for 3–4 minutes. Add the peppers, mushrooms and tomatoes, stir well and cook for 3 minutes.

Add the rice and stir to coat in the oil. Add a ladleful of hot stock and stir constantly until it is absorbed. Continue cooking in this way, adding a little hot stock at a time and stirring well between each addition. This will take 20–25 minutes.

Add the salami with the last ladleful of stock and stir well. The rice should be tender and creamy. Season to taste and sprinkle with Parmesan cheese to serve.

Sausage & lentil casserole

A superior sausage casserole that is good enough to serve at an informal dinner party. Serve with mashed potatoes and steamed Savoy cabbage.

Serves 4
Preparation time: 40 minutes
Cooking time: 35-40 minutes

1 tablespoon **olive oil**
450 g (1 lb) good quality **sausages**
1 **onion**, sliced
2 **garlic cloves**, crushed
1 teaspoon **ground allspice**
½ teaspoon freshly grated **nutmeg**
2 x 400 g cans **chopped tomatoes**
2 fresh **rosemary sprigs**, plus extra chopped leaves to garnish
2 **bay leaves**
200 ml (7 fl oz) **red wine**
100 g (3½ oz) **Puy lentils**

Heat the oil in a large lidded frying pan or flameproof casserole dish and cook the sausages for 5–8 minutes until nicely browned all over. Remove from the pan and set aside.

Add the onion and garlic to the pan and cook gently until the onion is softened. Stir in the allspice and nutmeg and mix well.

Pour in the tomatoes and bring to the boil. Simmer for 4–5 minutes to thicken slightly and then add the rosemary, bay leaves, red wine and Puy lentils. Stir in 200 ml (7 fl oz) of cold water, return the sausages to the pan and bring back up to the boil.

Cover the pan and reduce the heat. Simmer for 35–40 minutes until the lentils are tender. Stir several times during the cooking to prevent the lentils sticking to the base of the pan, and add a little more water if the sauce is becoming too thick. Remove the rosemary sprigs before serving garnished with a little chopped rosemary.

Venison casserole

This rich and tasty dish is also lovely made with fresh chestnuts (see Tip).
Serve with mashed potato and a selection of vegetables.

Serves 4–6
Preparation time:
25 minutes
Cooking time:
1½–1¾ hours

3 tablespoons **olive oil**
3 **shallots**, finely chopped
½ **onion**, finely chopped
4 rashers unsmoked **streaky**
   bacon, chopped
3 **celery sticks**, chopped
25 g (1 oz) **plain flour**
salt and freshly ground
   black pepper
675 g (1½ lb) **venison**, diced
425 ml (15 fl oz) **beef stock**
150 ml (5 fl oz) **red wine**
240 g can cooked peeled
   chestnuts
8 **juniper berries**, lightly
   crushed
3 tablespoons **Grand**
   Marnier

Preheat the oven to 160°C/320°F/Gas Mark 3.
Heat the oil in a large flameproof and
ovenproof casserole dish and fry the shallots
and onion gently until cooked. Stir in the bacon
and celery and cook for 3–4 minutes. Remove
to a plate with a slotted spoon and set aside.

Sift the flour into a shallow dish and season
well. Add the venison and turn to coat in the
seasoned flour. Add to the casserole dish and
fry until browned on all surfaces.

Return the onion, bacon and celery mixture
to the casserole. Stir in the stock and red
wine and bring to the boil. Add the chestnuts,
juniper berries and Grand Marnier.

Cover the casserole dish and cook in the oven
for 1½–1¾ hours or until the meat is tender.

Tip To prepare fresh chestnuts, make a slit
in each one, place in a pan of boiling water
and simmer for 10 minutes. Remove a couple
at a time and carefully remove the outer and
inner skin. If the inner skin remains, place
the chestnuts in fresh boiling water and boil
for a further 3 minutes, the skin will then rub
off easily.

Smoked haddock stew

This is a lovely recipe, halfway between a stew and a soup. It's very nourishing and filling. Serve with crusty bread.

Serves 4
Preparation time: 20 minutes
Cooking time: 20 minutes

225 g (8 oz) smoked **haddock fillet**
300 ml (10 fl oz) **boiling water**
1 tablespoon **sunflower oil**
1 **onion**, finely sliced
2 **celery sticks**, finely chopped
1 **carrot**, peeled and finely sliced
1 **potato**, peeled and finely diced
½ teaspoon **turmeric**
1 fresh **thyme sprig**
2 **bay leaves**
salt and freshly ground **black pepper**
300 ml (10 fl oz) **semi-skimmed milk**
75 g (2¾ oz) frozen **peas**
freshly grated **nutmeg**

Place the haddock in a large but shallow bowl and pour over the boiling water. Leave for 5 minutes and then drain, reserving the liquid.

Heat the oil in a large lidded saucepan and gently fry the onion for 2 minutes. Add the celery, carrot and potato and continue to fry for 2 more minutes.

Add half of the reserved fish liquid, the turmeric, thyme sprig and bay leaves and season. Bring to the boil and simmer very gently with the lid on until the vegetables are soft, about 15 minutes. Add the rest of the fish liquid, the milk and peas and cook for a further 3 minutes.

Gently flake in the fish, taking care to remove any skin and bones. Remove the bay leaves and thyme sprig and grate in a little nutmeg. Check the seasoning before serving.

Cod with bean mash

This is made in a frying pan with a lid. If your pan doesn't have a lid, improvise with a lid from a large saucepan, a baking tray or a piece of foil.

Serves 4
Preparation time: 10 minutes
Cooking time: 25 minutes

25 g (1 oz) unsalted **butter**
1 **leek**, thinly sliced, white and green parts kept separate
2 x 400 g cans **cannellini beans**, drained and rinsed
zest and juice of a **lemon**
450 ml (16 fl oz) **fish stock**
salt and freshly ground **black pepper**
1 teaspoon **wholegrain mustard**
4 smoked **cod loin pieces**, about 675 g (1½ lb) in total
3 tablespoons **crème fraîche**
4 tablespoons roughly chopped fresh **parsley**

Melt the butter in a large, lidded frying pan, add the green parts of the leek and fry gently for 2–3 minutes until just beginning to soften. Remove with a slotted spoon and set aside.

Add the white parts of the leek to the pan and fry for 2–3 minutes until softened. Add the cannellini beans, lemon zest and juice and stock. Season and bring to the boil. Cover and cook for 5 minutes.

Spread the mustard over the pieces of fish and season. Arrange on top of the bean mixture and cook for 8–10 minutes until just cooked and the fish flakes when pressed with a knife. Lift the fish out of the pan with a fish slice and keep hot on a plate.

Mash the beans coarsely and then stir in the softened green leeks, crème fraîche and parsley and heat through. Spoon on to plates and top with the fish.

Tomato & caraway prawns

This may seem an unusual combination, but it really works. Serve with a green salad and some crusty bread to mop up the juices.

Serves 4
Preparation time: 25 minutes
Cooking time: 20 minutes

2 tablespoons **olive oil**
2 **garlic cloves**, sliced finely
1 teaspoon **caraway seeds**
¼ teaspoon dried **chilli flakes**
1 **green pepper**, de-seeded and finely chopped
400 g can **chopped tomatoes**
a pinch of **caster sugar**
salt and freshly ground **black pepper**
350 g (12 oz) peeled cooked **prawns**, defrosted if frozen
1 tablespoon chopped fresh **coriander**, to garnish

Heat the oil in a large saucepan and fry the garlic until just golden. Add the caraway seeds, chilli flakes and green pepper, and stir well.

Add the tomatoes and sugar and season. Simmer for 20 minutes until the pepper is soft and the sauce thickened.

Add the prawns and reheat for 3 minutes. Serve immediately, sprinkled with the chopped coriander.

Provençal fish casserole

Many traditional Provençal dishes feature generous amounts of garlic. This uses just a couple of cloves, but if you prefer a stronger flavour, add more.

Serves 4
Preparation time:
  40 minutes
Cooking time:
  20–25 minutes

2–3 tablespoons **olive oil**
2 large **onions**, roughly chopped
2 **garlic cloves**, roughly chopped
2 tablespoons coarsely chopped fresh **parsley**, plus extra to garnish
450 g (1 lb) **tomatoes**, skinned and roughly chopped
125 ml (4 fl oz) **dry white wine**
1 teaspoon fresh or ½ teaspoon dried **marjoram**
salt and freshly ground **black pepper**
1 tablespoon **tomato purée**
4 **cod steaks** (approx 675 g/1½ lb total weight), skinned
50 g (1¾ oz) stoned **black olives**

Preheat the oven to 160°C/320°F/Gas Mark 3. Heat the oil in a large flameproof roasting tin and gently fry the onions, garlic and parsley over a low heat for 5–8 minutes.

Add the tomatoes, mix well and then stir in the wine and marjoram. Season and simmer, uncovered, for about 15 minutes. Stir in the tomato purée.

Place the cod steaks in the tin and cover with the sauce. Add the olives. Place the tin in the oven and cook for 20–25 minutes. Serve garnished with fresh parsley.

Variation Any firm-fleshed white fish such as monkfish or haddock can replace the cod in this dish.

Creamy fish pie

There's no fiddly sauce to make for these individual pies, just assemble the base and then top with mash.

Serves 4
Preparation time:
  30 minutes
Cooking time:
  20–25 minutes

550 g (1 lb 3 oz) **fish pie mix**
4 **spring onions**, thinly
  sliced
80 g (3 oz) frozen
  sweetcorn, just defrosted
zest of a small **lemon**
40 g (1½ oz) **Cheddar
  cheese**, grated
300 ml (10 fl oz) **double
  cream**
6 tablespoons **white wine**
  or **milk**
1 **garlic clove**, finely
  chopped (optional)
salt and freshly ground
  black pepper

Topping
800 g (1 lb 11 oz) **potatoes**,
  peeled and chopped
1 **egg**, beaten
3–4 tablespoons **milk**
80 g (3 oz) **Cheddar cheese**,
  grated

Preheat the oven to 200°C/400°F/Gas Mark 6. Combine the fish pie mix with the spring onions, sweetcorn, lemon zest and Cheddar cheese and divide between four 400 ml (14 fl oz) individual pie or ovenproof dishes.

Mix the cream, wine or milk and garlic, if using, together and season. Pour over the fish.

Bring a pan of water to the boil and cook the potatoes for 15 minutes until tender. Drain and mash with half the beaten egg and enough milk to make a smooth creamy mash. Season and mix with two-thirds of the Cheddar cheese.

Spoon the mash over the fish, brush with the remaining egg and sprinkle with the remaining cheese. Put the dishes on a baking tray and bake for 20–25 minutes until the top is golden and the fish base is bubbling and piping hot.

Tip If you are very short of time then cheat and use ready-made chilled mash from the supermarket.

Tuna stacks

Fresh tuna is a meaty fish and has quite a different flavour from the canned variety. This only needs a simple accompaniment of crusty bread.

Serves 4
Preparation time:
 20 minutes
Cooking time:
 45–60 minutes

1 **aubergine**, sliced
1 **onion**, chopped
2 **carrots**, peeled and thinly
 sliced
2 **courgettes**, sliced
4 **tomatoes**, quartered
salt and freshly ground
 black pepper
50 g (1¾ oz) unsalted **butter**
4 x 225–300 g (8–11 oz)
 tuna steaks

Topping
115 g (4¼ oz) **wholemeal
 breadcrumbs**
50 g (1¾ oz) **Cheddar
 cheese**, grated
1 **cooking apple**, cored
 and finely chopped

Preheat the oven to 180°C/350°F/Gas Mark 4. Place the aubergine, onion, carrots, courgettes and tomatoes in an ovenproof dish. Season well. Dot the vegetables with the butter and then place the tuna steaks on top.

In a small bowl, combine the topping ingredients and spread evenly over the fish. Bake for 45–60 minutes until the vegetables and fish are cooked.

Serve as a stack with the vegetables underneath the tuna.

Variation Salmon steaks can be used as an alternative.

Mussel & bacon chowder

Stretch a bag of mussels into a hearty supper for four by adding chunky pieces of potato and a creamy cider sauce. Delicious with warm bread.

Serves 4
Preparation time: 20 minutes
Cooking time: 30-35 minutes

1 kg (2 lb 4 oz) fresh **mussels**
1 tablespoon **olive oil**
80 g (3 oz) smoked **streaky bacon**, diced
25 g (1 oz) unsalted **butter**
450 g (1 lb) **potatoes**, peeled and cubed
6 **spring onions**, thinly sliced, white and green parts kept separate
1–2 **garlic cloves**, finely chopped
450 ml (16 fl oz) **fish stock**
150 ml (5 fl oz) **dry cider**
salt and freshly ground **black pepper**
150 ml (5 fl oz) **double cream**

Put the mussels in a large bowl, cover with cold water and set aside.

Heat the oil in a large lidded saucepan, add the bacon and fry for 3–4 minutes, stirring until lightly browned. Add the butter and, when melted, stir in the potatoes and white parts of the spring onions. Fry for 3–4 minutes and then add the garlic, stock and cider. Season lightly. Bring to the boil, cover and simmer gently for 10–15 minutes until the potatoes are tender.

Meanwhile, clean the mussels. Take out one a time from the bowl of cold water, scrub those that are tightly shut with a small brush under a slowly running cold tap to remove any dirt or barnacles and pull off the hairy fibrous strands or 'beard'. Discard any mussels that are open and add the prepared mussels to a fresh bowl of cold water.

When the potatoes are cooked, stir in the cream, drain the mussels, add to the pan and sprinkle with the green parts of the spring onions. Cover and cook over a medium heat for 10 minutes until the mussel shells have opened. Ladle into large bowls to serve.

Bean & vegetable hotpot

Easy to make, this colourful dish is good with naan bread, rice or a jacket potato. The flavour is even better if stored in the fridge for a day or two.

Serves 6
Preparation time: 15 minutes
Cooking time: 1½–1¾ hours

1 small **aubergine**, sliced and larger slices halved
1 tablespoon **lemon juice**
2 **garlic cloves**, finely chopped
1 large **onion**, chopped
1 **red pepper**, de-seeded and finely diced
1 **yellow pepper**, de-seeded and finely diced
1 **green pepper**, de-seeded and finely diced
400 g can **kidney beans**, drained and rinsed
2 x 400 g cans **chopped tomatoes with herbs**
2 tablespoons fresh or 2 teaspoons dried **basil**
2 **courgettes**, sliced
225 g (8 oz) frozen **sweetcorn**
freshly ground **black pepper**

Brush the aubergine slices with the lemon juice to prevent browning.

Put the garlic, onion, peppers, kidney beans, tomatoes and basil into a large lidded saucepan. Cover, bring to the boil and simmer for 30 minutes, until the vegetables are beginning to soften.

Add the courgettes and aubergine, bring back to the boil and simmer for a further 45–60 minutes.

Add the sweetcorn, bring back to the boil and simmer for 5 minutes. Season to taste with black pepper.

Tip If you wish, add 4 tablespoons of port with the sweetcorn.

Squash & rocket risotto

Full of fibre, pearl barley makes a change from the more usual rice-based risotto. If you don't like blue cheese, use Parmesan instead.

Serves 4
Preparation time:
 15 minutes
Cooking time:
 65–70 minutes

40 g (1½ oz) unsalted **butter**
1 tablespoon **olive oil**
1 **onion**, thinly sliced
200 g (7 oz) **pearl barley**
1 litre (1¾ pints) **vegetable
 stock**
salt and freshly ground
 black pepper
450 g (1 lb) **butternut
 squash**, peeled,
 de-seeded and diced
50 g (1¾ oz) **blue cheese**,
 crumbled

To garnish
25 g (1 oz) **rocket**
3 tablespoons **pine nuts**,
 lightly toasted
crumbled **blue cheese**
 (optional)

Heat the butter and oil in a large lidded saucepan, add the onion and fry gently for 5 minutes, stirring occasionally until just beginning to colour.

Stir in the pearl barley and stock and season. Bring to the boil, cover and simmer gently for 40 minutes.

Stir in the butternut squash, cover again and cook for a further 25–30 minutes until the squash is tender, stirring from time to time and more frequently towards the end of cooking as the barley absorbs more of the stock.

Stir in the cheese, spoon into large shallow bowls and top with the rocket, pine nuts and a little extra cheese, if using.

Coconut vegetable curry

This is a straightforward vegetable curry. You can make it hotter by adding an extra chilli or more curry paste. Serve with rice or naan bread.

Serves 4
**Preparation and
    cooking time: 1 hour**

1 **onion**, chopped
1 **potato**, peeled and
    chopped
1 small **aubergine**, chopped
1 **carrot**, peeled and
    chopped
1 small **red pepper**,
    de-seeded and chopped
1 small **green pepper**,
    de-seeded and chopped
2 **garlic cloves**, crushed
1 **green** or **red chilli**,
    de-seeded and finely
    chopped
2.5 cm (1 inch) fresh **root
    ginger**, finely chopped
2 tablespoons good quality
    curry paste (medium or
    hot)
75 g (2¾ oz) **creamed
    coconut**, chopped
juice of ½ a **lemon**
2 tablespoons chopped
    fresh **coriander**
salt and freshly ground
    black pepper

Put all the vegetables in a large saucepan with the garlic, chilli and ginger. Cover with about 300–350 ml (10–12 fl oz) of water. Bring to the boil and stir in the curry paste.

Simmer gently until the vegetables are tender, about 20 minutes, adding a little more water if needed.

Add the creamed coconut, stirring gently to mix and then add the lemon juice and coriander. Check the seasoning and serve.

Vegetable korma

Serves 4
**Preparation and
   cooking time: 1 hour**

1 **potato**, peeled and cubed
2 **carrots**, peeled and cubed
10–12 **cauliflower florets**
1 **green pepper**, de-seeded
   and cubed
100 g (3½ oz) **peas**
100 g (3½ oz) **green beans**
2 tablespoons **vegetable oil**
1 teaspoon **mustard seeds**
1 **onion**, sliced
3 **garlic cloves**, crushed
2.5 cm (1 inch) fresh **root
   ginger**, finely chopped
2 tablespoons **desiccated
   coconut**
400 g can **chopped
   tomatoes**
400 g (14 oz) **natural yogurt**
1 teaspoon **garam masala**
1 teaspoon **ground
   coriander**
1 teaspoon **ground cumin**
¼–½ teaspoon **chilli
   powder**
½ teaspoon **turmeric**
50 g (1¾ oz) **ground almonds**
salt and freshly ground
   black pepper
chopped fresh **coriander**,
   to garnish

Bring a large saucepan of water to the boil and add the potato, carrots and cauliflower. Simmer for 5 minutes. Add the green pepper, peas and beans, bring back up to simmering point and cook for a further 3–4 minutes. Drain the vegetables and set aside.

Heat the oil in the pan and stir in the mustard seeds. When they start to pop, add the onion, garlic and ginger and cook gently for 5–6 minutes to soften the onion. Stir in the desiccated coconut and cook for a further minute and then add the chopped tomatoes.

Meanwhile, mix together the yogurt, spices and ground almonds.

Add the vegetables to the onion and tomato mixture. Lower the heat and carefully stir in the spiced yoghurt. Stir carefully to combine the sauce with the vegetables and simmer gently for a further 8–10 minutes until the vegetables are completely tender. If you prefer a slightly thinner sauce, stir in up to 100 ml (3½ fl oz) of water.

Check the seasoning and serve with a sprinkling of chopped coriander leaves.

Tip If you have a mill to grind the desiccated coconut to a finer texture, it improves the look of the sauce.

Vegetable satay stir-fry

A tasty combination of crunchy stir-fried vegetables in a spicy peanut sauce makes a satisfying vegetarian main course.

Serves 4
Preparation time:
  20 minutes
Cooking time:
  10 minutes

80 g (3 oz) **green beans**, cut into 5 cm (2 inch) pieces
115 g (4¼ oz) **broccoli**, sliced diagonally
2 tablespoons **vegetable oil**
2 **garlic cloves**, sliced
4 thin slices fresh **root ginger**
1 **red chilli**, de-seeded and finely sliced
115 g (4¼ oz) **mangetout**
2 **celery sticks**, sliced diagonally
50 g (1¾ oz) **courgettes** cut into strips
150 ml (5 fl oz) **vegetable stock**
4 tablespoons smooth **peanut butter**
50 g (1¾ oz) roasted salted **peanuts**
salt and freshly ground **black pepper**

Bring a large shallow pan of water to the boil, add the beans and broccoli and blanch for 30 seconds. Drain and refresh in cold water, drain again.

Heat the oil in the pan, add the garlic, ginger and chilli and stir fry to release the flavours.

Reduce the heat, add the mangetout to the pan and stir fry for 1 minute. Add the celery, courgettes, broccoli and beans to the pan and stir fry for another minute until the vegetables are cooked but still crisp and bright green.

Stir in the vegetable stock and peanut butter and heat through until bubbling. Add the peanuts, season and simmer for 2 minutes. Serve immediately.

Spicy Moroccan vegetables

Seven vegetables are used in this dish, as seven is considered a lucky number in Morocco. Choose from those listed and serve with couscous.

Serves 6
**Preparation and
   cooking time:
   1½ hours**

1 tablespoon **olive oil**
1 **onion**, chopped
400 g can **chopped
   tomatoes**
1 vegetable **stock cube**
1 **garlic clove**, crushed
½ teaspoon dried **chilli
   flakes**
1 teaspoon **ground cumin**
salt and freshly ground
   black pepper
2 tablespoons chopped
   fresh **parsley**

Vegetables
225 g (8 oz) **new potatoes**
2 **carrots**
1 small **white cabbage**
1 **turnip**
1 **parsnip**
175 g (6 oz) **broad beans**
4 **celery sticks**
1 small **aubergine**
1 small **sweet potato**
½ **butternut squash**

Choose six vegetables from those listed (the onion is the seventh) and prepare them, peeling, de-seeding and cutting into chunks where necessary.

Heat the oil in a large saucepan and fry the onion until golden. Add the tomatoes, stock cube, garlic, chilli flakes and cumin. Season, add 300 ml (10 fl oz) of water, and bring to the boil.

Add whichever six vegetables you are using in rotation, starting with the new potatoes, carrots or cabbage. Cover and simmer for 10 minutes.

Next add the turnip, parsnip, broad beans or celery and cook for a further 10 minutes. Lastly add the aubergine, sweet potato or squash and cook for another 10 minutes.

Serve sprinkled with the parsley.

Tip The secret is to cook whichever vegetables you select in the right order, so follow the sequence of cooking given here.

Lentil & vegetable curry

Serve this really simple curry as a main course for four with garlic and coriander naan bread or as an accompanying vegetable dish for eight.

Serves 4
**Preparation time:
  20 minutes**
Cooking time: 1 hour

2 tablespoons **vegetable oil**
1 **onion**, finely chopped
2 **garlic cloves**, crushed
2 tablespoons **curry powder**
1 teaspoon **turmeric**
6 **cardamom pods**, crushed
½ teaspoon **ground
  cinnamon**
2 **bay leaves**
115 g (4¼ oz) **red lentils**,
  rinsed well
1 **aubergine**, cubed
2 **carrots**, peeled and sliced
1 **cauliflower**, divided into
  small florets
175 g (6 oz) **okra**, each cut
  into 3
3 tablespoons chopped
  fresh **coriander**

To garnish
4 tablespoons **natural
  yogurt**
mango chutney

Heat the oil in a large lidded saucepan and fry the onion and garlic until soft. Add the spices and bay leaves and cook for 1 minute. Add the lentils, aubergine, carrots and cauliflower and cook for 5 minutes.

Pour in 850 ml (1½ pints) of water and bring to the boil. Reduce to a gentle simmer, cover and cook gently for 1 hour.

Add the okra and coriander and cook for 5 minutes. Serve garnished with the yogurt swirled with a little mango chutney.

Oriental mushrooms

Mushrooms are a good source of protein and are extremely low in calories as long as they are not cooked in rich, creamy sauces.

Serves 4
Preparation time:
   20 minutes
Cooking time:
   10 minutes

1 tablespoon **vegetable oil**
2 **garlic cloves**, chopped
125 g (4½ oz) **shiitake mushrooms**, thickly sliced
125 g (4½ oz) **oyster mushrooms**, thickly sliced
200 g (7 oz) **chestnut mushrooms**, quartered
1 tablespoon **soy sauce**
1 tablespoon **dry sherry**
3 tablespoons **oyster sauce**
1 teaspoon **soft light brown sugar**
100 ml (3½ fl oz) hot **vegetable stock**
a bunch of **spring onions**, chopped
200 g (7 oz) **bean sprouts**
300 g (10½ oz) 'straight to wok' **noodles**

Heat the vegetable oil in a wok or large frying pan and stir fry the garlic for 30 seconds; do not allow it to brown. Add all the mushrooms and stir fry for 1 minute, tossing and mixing well.

Add the soy sauce, sherry, oyster sauce, sugar and hot vegetable stock. Reduce the heat slightly and simmer for 4–5 minutes until the mushrooms are just tender.

Stir in the spring onions, bean sprouts and noodles. Continue cooking for 2 minutes to warm the noodles thoroughly. Serve immediately in warm bowls.

Mushrooms in red wine

Serve poured over plain Quorn fillets, stir fried tofu or steamed individual cauliflowers. It is also excellent over beef or turkey steaks.

Serves 3
Preparation time:
  10 minutes
Cooking time:
  40 minutes

25 g (1 oz) unsalted **butter**
1 **red onion**, finely chopped
110 g (4 oz) **button mushrooms**, sliced
55 g (2 oz) **chestnut mushrooms**, sliced
55 g (2 oz) **oyster mushrooms**, sliced
4 tablespoons **brandy**
200 ml (7 fl oz) **red wine**
2 teaspoons **plain flour** or **cornflour**
150 ml (5 fl oz) hot **vegetable stock**
freshly ground **black pepper**

Heat the butter in a lidded heavy-based pan, add the onion, cover and cook over a gentle heat until tender, this should take about 20 minutes. Remove with a slotted spoon and set aside.

Add the mushrooms to the pan and stir fry for 2 minutes over a medium heat. Add the brandy, bring to the boil and simmer without a lid for 1–2 minutes, until the liquid is reduced by half. Pour in the red wine, return the onion to the pan and simmer for 5 minutes.

Mix the flour or cornflour with a little cold water and blend to a smooth paste. Stir the stock into the paste. Pour the blended stock into the pan and bring to the boil, stirring all the time.

Simmer gently for about 15 minutes, until the sauce has a syrupy consistency. Season to taste with black pepper.

Beetroot chilli

Preparing beetroot can be a messy business, so don a pair of rubber gloves before you begin to avoid pink hands. Serve with soft tortillas or rice.

Serves 4
Preparation time:
45 minutes
Cooking time:
45 minutes

2 tablespoons **sunflower oil**
1 **onion**, chopped
200 g (7 oz) **button mushrooms**, halved
2 **garlic cloves**, finely chopped
1 teaspoon dried **chilli flakes**
1 teaspoon **ground cumin**
½ teaspoon **ground cinnamon**
500 g (1 lb 2 oz) **beetroot**, peeled and cut into 2 cm (¾ inch) dice
400 g can **kidney beans**, drained and rinsed
400 g can **chopped tomatoes**
1 tablespoon **light muscovado sugar**
450 ml (16 fl oz) **vegetable stock**
salt and freshly ground **black pepper**

Heat the oil in a large lidded saucepan, add the onion and fry for 5 minutes, stirring from time to time until softened. Add the mushrooms and garlic and fry for 5 minutes.

Add the chilli flakes, cumin, cinnamon, beetroot, kidney beans, tomatoes, sugar and stock and season well. Bring to the boil, stirring.

Cover and simmer gently for 45 minutes, stirring from time to time and topping up with a little extra stock if needed until the beetroot is tender. Serve.

Tip Serve garnished with soured cream and a tomato salsa made from 2 diced tomatoes, 3 finely chopped spring onions and a small bunch of chopped fresh coriander leaves.

Chestnut gratin

Serves 4
**Preparation and
  cooking time:
  65–70 minutes**

2 tablespoons **olive oil**
1 **red onion**, chopped
1 **aubergine**, cut into 2 cm
  (¾ inch) cubes
2 **leeks**, thickly sliced
2 **celery sticks**, thickly
  sliced
½ teaspoon **ground ginger**
½ teaspoon freshly grated
  nutmeg
a large pinch of **ground
  cloves**
1 tablespoon **plain flour**
250 ml (8 fl oz) **vegetable
  stock**
150 ml (5 fl oz) **red wine**
1 tablespoon **tomato purée**
salt and freshly ground
  black pepper
240 g can peeled cooked
  chestnuts

Topping
50 g (1¾ oz) **crusty bread**,
  torn into small pieces
2 fresh **rosemary sprigs**,
  leaves roughly chopped
25 g (1 oz) fresh **Parmesan
  cheese**, grated
1 tablespoon **olive oil**

Preheat the oven to 190°C/375°F/Gas Mark 5.
Heat the oil in a shallow, lidded, flameproof
and ovenproof casserole dish, add the onion
and aubergine and fry for 5 minutes, stirring
until just beginning to soften and brown. Add
the leeks, celery and spices and cook for
1 minute.

Sprinkle the flour over the top and stir the
vegetables to mix. Pour over the stock and
red wine and then mix in the tomato purée.
Season. Add the chestnuts, cover and simmer
gently for 10 minutes.

Mix the bread for the topping with the
rosemary and Parmesan. Remove the lid from
the casserole dish, sprinkle the crumbs over
the top and drizzle with the oil. Bake,
uncovered, for 20–25 minutes until golden.

Summer vegetable risotto

Risottos make very simple yet elegant meals and are not as difficult to cook successfully as many believe. Accompany with a crisp salad, if desired.

Serves 4
Preparation time:
  15 minutes
Cooking time:
  30 minutes

1 tablespoon **olive oil**
1 **onion**, chopped
2 **garlic cloves**, chopped
100 g (3½ oz) **asparagus tips**
1 **courgette**, sliced
350 g (12 oz) **risotto rice**
300 ml (10 fl oz) **dry white wine**
1 litre (1¾ pints) hot **vegetable stock**
125 g (4½ oz) shelled **broad beans**, defrosted if frozen
2 ripe **tomatoes**, de-seeded and chopped
2 tablespoons chopped fresh **parsley**, plus extra to garnish
1 tablespoon roughly torn fresh **basil**, plus tiny leaves to garnish
25 g (1 oz) **Parmesan cheese**, grated
freshly ground **black pepper**

Heat the oil in a large frying pan and gently cook the onion and garlic for 3–4 minutes until softened but not coloured. Transfer to a plate using a slotted spoon. Add the asparagus tips and courgette slices to the pan and cook for 3–4 minutes. Remove to the plate and keep warm.

Add the risotto rice and cook for about 1 minute, stirring, to allow the grains to become coated with the oil. Pour in the wine, bring up to the boil and then reduce the heat and simmer gently, stirring until the wine has been absorbed.

Add half the hot vegetable stock and bring to the boil. Again, reduce the heat and simmer gently, stirring until the stock is absorbed. Add half of the remaining stock along with the broad beans. Bring to the boil and then allow to simmer gently until the liquid is absorbed.

Add the last of the stock and bring to the boil, Simmer gently until the stock is absorbed and the rice is tender. The risotto should be thick and creamy with the grains of rice soft but still retaining a little bite.

Stir in the tomatoes, herbs and reserved vegetables, along with the Parmesan and some black pepper. Mix gently. Remove from the heat, cover the pan and leave to stand for 4–5 minutes to allow the flavours to mix. Serve on warmed plates, garnished with the extra herbs.

Squash & lentil casserole

Ginger gives a warm flavour to this casserole, making it ideal for cold winter days. Serve with steamed rice if you wish.

Serves 4
Preparation time:
  15 minutes
Cooking time:
  40-45 minutes

1 tablespoon **vegetable oil**
1 **onion**, sliced
1 **garlic clove**, crushed
2.5 cm (1 inch) fresh **root ginger**, grated
1 **butternut squash**, peeled, de-seeded and chopped
1 **yellow pepper**, de-seeded and cubed
½ teaspoon **ground cumin**
1 teaspoon **ground coriander**
150 ml (5 fl oz) **vegetable stock**
400 g can **chopped tomatoes**
400 g can **lentils**, drained and rinsed
400 g can **cannellini beans**, drained and rinsed
100 g (3½ oz) **baby spinach leaves**, washed
1 tablespoon chopped fresh **coriander**
freshly ground **black pepper**

Heat the oil in a large flameproof casserole dish or a saucepan and gently cook the onion for 4–5 minutes until beginning to soften. Add the garlic and ginger and cook for a further 2–3 minutes.

Stir in the butternut squash, pepper, cumin and coriander and sauté gently for 5 minutes. Add the stock and tomatoes and bring up to the boil. Reduce the heat, cover the pan and simmer for 20–25 minutes until the butternut squash is tender.

Add the lentils and beans, stir through and continue to cook for a further 5 minutes until the beans are thoroughly warmed through. Add the spinach and coriander and stir through for 3 minutes until the spinach is wilted. Season to taste with black pepper and serve immediately.

Index